COOKING WITH QUALITY BRITISH CHICKEN

Colour Library Books

INTRODUCTION

Chicken makes a major contribution to a healthy diet, since it is high in protein, rich in important vitamins and low in fat. In addition, it tastes delicious and its flavour combines well with almost every herb, spice, fruit or vegetable you can imagine. It is also excellent value for money. So it's not surprising that chicken is the most popular meat in Britain today.

In the old days you would choose your own chicken, judging it by its beak and feet and feeling the plumpness of the breast, before it was dressed for you. Today, most of us have to rely on someone else to ensure these standards are maintained on our behalf and that's why Quality British Chicken was formed in 1984.

Quality British Chicken was a founder member of Food From Britain's quality food mark scheme. It is now the most successful food mark in the shops today.

The Quality British Chicken scheme covers whole chickens, both fresh and frozen, chicken portions, poussins and also corn-fed and extra large chickens. Its standards are stringent and cover everything from the raising of the bird to its eventual packaging and distribution. To ensure that such high standards can be guaranteed, the scheme is very well policed. All products carrying the Quality British Chicken symbol are checked regularly on a national basis by independent Food From Britain inspectors, and members of the scheme are inspected ten times a year. Random checks are also made to see that standards are being maintained, and members have to reapply for membership annually.

Thus the red, white and blue Quality British Chicken symbol provides you with the reassurance that the chicken you are buying has been reared to rigidly set standards and has passed a whole range of tests for quality. These remain consistent all year round, guaranteeing that British is indeed best.

So, whether your recipe calls for a whole chicken or for portions, if you choose Quality British Chicken, you'll know that you're getting the best.

Photography by Peter Barry
Recipes Prepared and Styled by Bridgeen Deery and Wendy Devenish
Designed by Dick Richardson

CLB 2024
This edition published 1990
© 1989 Colour Library Books Ltd., Godalming, Surrey.
Printed in Belgium by Casterman.
All rights reserved.
ISBN 0 86283 762 6

ROAST CHICKEN WITH GARLIC AND HERB SAUCE

SERVES 4

This dinner party dish is extremely impressive and yet very easy. The stunning sauce is literally whisked up in seconds but tastes as though you've taken the day off work to prepare it.

1 x 1.35kg/3lb oven-ready Quality British
   Chicken
1 large and 1 small Boursin cheese with garlic
and herbs
1 medium-sized lemon
2 small bay leaves

1. Grate the lemon zest directly into a small bowl and mash up all the large Boursin evenly with this.

2. Ease this mixture evenly and gently between the breast and the skin of the bird.

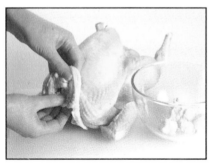

STEP 2

3. Put the two bay leaves into the chicken cavity and put the chicken into a roasting bag.

4. Squeeze the lemon and pour the juice into the bag; put the lemon halves into the cavity of the chicken.

5. Seal and slash as directed and bake at 190°C/375°F/Gas Mark 5 for 20 minutes per lb, plus 20 minutes extra.

6. Cut the bag and pour all the juices, including those inside the chicken, into a measuring jug.

STEP 6

7. Now carefully pour away the fat which will have risen to the top until you have about ¼ pint of well-flavoured stock. Reheat gently and then remove from heat.

8. Chop the small Boursin into pieces and whisk into the warm sauce.

STEP 8

9. Carve the chicken and pour on the sauce immediately.

Cook's Notes

🕐 TIME: Preparation takes about 20 minutes, cooking takes about 1 hour and 20 minutes.

○ SERVING IDEAS: A chilled rosé wine from Provence is an excellent accompaniment to this dish.

❓ VARIATION: You could try ringing the changes by using pepper-flavoured Boursin or by combining two flavours, using one for the stuffing and one for the sauce.

SUMMER PICNIC PARMESAN AND HERB CHICKEN

SERVES 4

This dish is fabulous served cold, when the flavours have had time to mingle and develop. It is also good served warm – especially in summer – with a chilled dry rosé wine from Provence.

---

1 x 1.35kg/3lb oven-ready Quality British Chicken
50g/2oz Parmesan cheese, grated
25g/1oz ground almonds
4 tbsps olive oil
25g/1oz fresh garlic, or rather less if old
15g/½ oz fresh basil
1 tbsp extra Parmesan

---

1. Mix together the cheese, almonds and oil to form a soft paste. Finely slice the garlic, chop the basil very roughly and stir these into the paste.

2. Gently ease the chicken skin away from the flesh, starting around the wishbone (which you can remove to facilitate carving).

STEP 2

3. Press the stuffing under the skin as evenly as you can, covering the whole of the breast and some of the legs.

STEP 3

4. Pat the skin back over the bird.

5. Rub the extra Parmesan into the skin before putting the bird into a roasting bag, or a roasting dish which you can cover with a lid or foil.

STEP 5

6. Bake at 190°C/375°F/Gas Mark 5 for 20 minutes per lb, plus 20 minutes extra.

Cook's Notes

⏱ TIME: Preparation takes about 25 minutes, cooking takes about 1 hour and 20 minutes.

◯ SERVING IDEAS: Serve with a lovely, crisp, green salad.

❓ VARIATION: Substitute any fresh herb like mint or parsley for the basil – the dish will be equally delicious.

CHICKEN THIGHS OR DRUMSTICKS IN TOMATO SAUCE

SERVES 4

Such an easy dish and so adaptable – use whatever fresh herbs you have available.

8 Quality British Chicken thighs, or drumsticks
2 tbsps oil
25g/1oz butter
400g/14oz can crushed tomatoes
At least 4 tbsps chopped fresh herbs, including
    2 tbsps parsley with marjoram, mint, oregano,
    basil, thyme, etc
1 tsp finely grated lemon zest
Lemon juice to taste
Salt and freshly ground black pepper

1. Wipe over the chicken pieces with some kitchen paper.

2. Heat the oil with the butter and brown the chicken over a moderate heat, turning frequently and taking care not to let the butter burn. Drain off any excess fat.

STEP 2

3. Add the tomatoes, half the fresh herbs and the lemon zest, stir well, cover the pan and simmer for 20-25 minutes, until the chicken is really tender.

STEP 3

4. Stir in the remaining herbs until they turn a bright green colour and you can smell their oils. Check seasoning, adding lemon juice, salt and pepper to taste.

STEP 4

5. Serve with rice or pasta, sprinkled with extra fresh herbs.

Cook's Notes

TIME: Preparation takes about 25 minutes, cooking takes about 1 hour and 20 minutes.

VARIATION: Although not included, garlic is always successful when added to anything herb flavoured

TOMATO POUSSINS WITH CORIANDER

SERVES 4

A wonderful combination of flavours makes this an excellent dinner party dish.

4 oven-ready Quality British Chicken poussins
1 sachet powdered saffron
225g/8oz can tomatoes, whole or chopped
2 large cloves garlic
50g/2oz butter
25g/1oz fresh coriander, leaves and stalks
Salt and freshly ground black pepper

1. Trim the birds of any loose skin and parson's noses.

STEP 1

2. Dissolve the saffron in a little of the juice from the tomatoes and paint the birds all over with this. Take care when handling saffron, as it stains – ideally, wear a pair of rubber gloves.

STEP 2

3. Fold the coriander a few times, chop roughly and put most of it into the cavities of the birds.

STEP 3

4. Put the birds into a baking dish just large enough to accommodate them, with the tomatoes.

5. Squeeze the garlic juice over them, then dot with butter and sprinkle with the remaining coriander.

6. Season lightly with salt and pepper, turn the birds onto their sides and cover the dish with a dome of foil.

7. Bake in a preheated oven, 180°C/350°F/Gas Mark 4, for 30 minutes, or until the birds are completely cooked, turning them onto their other side halfway through the cooking time.

Cook's Notes

TIME: Preparation takes about 25 minutes, cooking takes about 1 hour and 20 minutes.

SERVING IDEAS: Serve on a bed of plain rice or on potatoes boiled in their skins and roughly chopped.

CHINESE LEAF CHICKEN
STIR-FRY SALAD

SERVES 4

A more substantial version of the warm salads which many restaurants serve as a first course.

4 tbsps olive oil
3 cloves garlic, crushed
450g/1lb Quality British Chicken breast,
    skinned and cut into 1cm/½-inch-wide strips
225g/8oz Chinese leaves, shredded
½ cucumber, cut into 4cm/2 inch sticks
1 green pepper, cut into thin 4cm/2 inch strips
2 sticks celery, cut into thin 4cm/2 inch strips
2-3 tbsps dry vermouth
Salt and freshly ground black pepper
1 tbsp parsley

1. Heat three tablespoons of the oil and stir-fry the garlic and chicken breast over a medium high heat until tender and lightly browned but cooked through. This should take about 10 minutes. Remove the chicken and keep warm.

2. Add the Chinese leaves, cucumber, pepper and celery to the pan with the remaining oil and stir-fry for 2-3 minutes.

STEP 2

3. Turn the mixture onto a heated serving dish or individual plates, then arrange the chicken on top.

4. Add the parsley and vermouth to the pan and scrape any sediment from the bottom. Season, pour over the chicken and vegetables and serve at once.

STEP 1

STEP 4

Cook's Notes

⏱ TIME: Preparation takes about 5 minutes, cooking takes about 15 minutes.

❓ VARIATION: Courgettes can be substituted for the cucumber.

◎ SERVING IDEAS: Serve as a warm salad amongst 6 or 8, or as an attractive dinner or lunch for fewer. It is essential that your guests are waiting at the table or the fresh crunch of the green vegetables, in contrast with the succulent chicken, will be lost.

PLUM-GLAZED CHICKEN WINGS

SERVES 4

This dish is extremely versatile. It can be cooked under the grill, in the oven or on the barbecue, and is delicious hot or cold.

8 Quality British Chicken wings
½ onion, sliced
2-3 cloves garlic, chopped
1 bay leaf
2 star anise (a Chinese spice available in most good
    supermarkets)

Glaze
3 heaped tbsps plum jam
1 tsp five spice powder
1 tbsp vinegar, cider or wine

1. Put the chicken wings in a saucepan together with the onion, garlic, bay leaf and 2 star anise.

STEP 2

2. Cover with cold water, bring to the boil and simmer for 10 minutes.

3. Mix together the jam, five spice powder and vinegar, cider or wine.

STEP 3

4. Put the drained wings on to the rack of a grill pan and paint with half the jam mixture. Grill under a high heat for 10 minutes, basting several times.

STEP 4

5. Turn the wings, brush with the remaining jam and continue cooking for a further 10 minutes until very brown, taking care not to let the jam burn. Alternatively, the wings may be cooked in the oven at 220°C/425°F/Gas Mark 7 for 15 minutes, then for a further 15 minutes after the second coating of jam.

6. Serve the wings hot or cold. If cooking these for a barbecue, do be very careful not to serve them immediately as the jam gets very hot and will burn unwary mouths.

Cook's Notes

TIME: Preparation takes about 10 minutes, cooking takes about 30 minutes.

SERVING IDEAS: For a barbecue, a great accompaniment would be hot jacket potatoes with butter. Alternatively, serve on a bed of plain boiled rice.

MANGO CHICKEN THIGHS OR DRUMSTICKS WITH COCONUT

SERVES 4

Slightly piquant and immensely satisfying and simple to make. Ideal cold in picnic hampers.

8 Quality British Chicken thighs or drumsticks
175g/6oz mango chutney
1 tsp mild curry paste
25g/1oz desiccated coconut
Lemon juice

1. Skin the chicken pieces and with a sharp knife make a 2cm/1 inch slit along the bone.

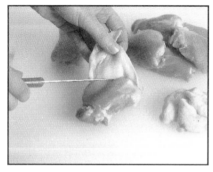

STEP 1

2. Cut the flesh each side of the bone to make two small pockets, but don't cut all the way through.

3. Put the mango chutney into a sieve standing over a bowl and separate the solids from the sauce.

4. Chop the mango flesh roughly, mix with the coconut and curry paste and add a squeeze of lemon juice.

5. Stuff the pockets with the mixture and place them in a lightly oiled or greased baking dish.

STEP 5

6. Stir a squeeze of lemon juice into the reserved sauce from the mango chutney and brush half of this over the thighs.

STEP 6

7. Preheat the oven to 200°C/400°F/Gas Mark 6. Bake uncovered for 15 minutes, then brush with the remaining sauce and return to the oven for a further 15 minutes, or until cooked.

Cook's Notes

TIME: Preparation takes about 15 minutes, cooking takes about 30 minutes.

VARIATION: This recipe can be varied by using peach chutney or any other chutney that has large, solid pieces of fruit in it.

SERVING IDEAS: Choose the thighs if you are eating at table, perhaps with a salad as either a first or main course. The drumsticks are also ideal for picnics and buffets.

CHICKEN AND SHRIMPS WITH PASTA IN A CREAM SAUCE

SERVES 4

Here we have the always successful combination of chicken and seafood. It is important that the outer skin of each shelled broad bean is removed to reveal the tender, brilliant green internal goodies which so complement the appearance of the dish.

450g/1lb boneless Quality British Chicken breasts
6 tbsps white wine
Salt and freshly ground pepper
175g/6oz shelled broad beans (before removing outer skins)
50g/2oz potted shrimps
25g/1oz (scant) plain flour
300ml/½ pint single cream
1 heaped tbsp chopped fresh dill or 1 tsp dried dill

---

1. Cut the chicken breasts into strips about 2cm/¾ inch wide, put them into a shallow ovenproof dish, pour over the wine and season with salt and pepper.

STEP 1

2. Cover and cook in a preheated oven for about 25 minutes at 180°C/350°F/Gas Mark 4, until tender. Allow to cool, then cut the strips in half lengthwise.

3. Strain and reserve the cooking liquid.

4. Cook the beans until just tender, then drain and remove the white outer skins. (If you use frozen broad beans the skins can be slipped off before cooking, as the beans have already been blanched.)

5. Melt the potted shrimps over a gentle heat then stir in the flour and blend carefully. Continue cooking for 1-2 minutes, stirring constantly.

STEP 5

6. Make the ½ pint single cream up to ¾ pint using the reserved cooking liquid. Off the heat, stir this into the floured shrimps and return to a low heat, stirring until you have a smooth sauce.

7. Add the dill and the shelled beans and season to taste. Stir in the chicken strips, heat gently until warmed and serve with pasta.

STEP 7

Cook's Notes

TIME: Preparation takes about 15 minutes, cooking takes about 30 minutes.

VARIATION: This recipe can be made with ready-cooked chicken.

SERVING IDEAS: Serve with a green side salad. A chilled white Alsace wine always complements pasta.

SAFFRON CHICKEN PIE

SERVES 4

The exciting contrast of rich chicken and warm spices with the sharpness of lemon and parsley is bridged by a sprinkle of sugar.

350g/12oz uncooked Quality British Chicken
    meat, cut into long, generous strips
22.5-25 × 5cm/9-10 × 2 inch pie dish, lined with
    rich shortcrust pastry and baked blind
50g/2oz butter
50g/2oz onion, finely chopped
6 tbsps lemon juice
3 sachets powdered saffron
8 eggs, beaten
2 tsps ground cinnamon
15g/½ oz fresh parsley, including stalks,
    coarsely chopped
½ tsp white pepper
1 tsp sugar

---

1. To bake blind, line the pastry case with foil or greaseproof paper and cover with baking beans (you can buy ceramic ones or use dried kidney beans and throw them away afterwards). Put into a preheated oven, 200°C/400°F/Gas Mark 6, and bake for 10 minutes. Remove from oven, remove the beans, carefully take off the foil/greaseproof paper and return to the oven for a further ten minutes until the base is set.

2. Once the pastry has been blind baked, lightly whisk a white from one of the eggs and paint this on to the hot pastry; return to the oven for a few minutes to ensure it sets and thus seals the pastry for you.

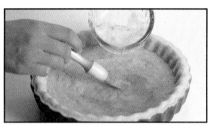

STEP 2

3. Melt the butter, add the onion, lemon juice and saffron and cook gently until the onion is really soft.

STEP 3

4. Stir in the chicken meat, cook gently for 5 minutes then set aside to cool.

5. Beat the cinnamon and white pepper into the eggs and stir in the parsley and all the juices from the cooked chicken.

6. Arrange the chicken neatly on the cooled pastry case and ladle on the egg mixture. Transfer to a preheated oven, 160°C/325°F/Gas Mark 3, for 15 minutes.

7. Sprinkle with sugar and return to the oven for a further 25 minutes, until lightly browned just around the edges and only just set – it will firm up more once out of the oven. (If you overcook the pie, the eggs will toughen.) Serve warm or cold.

Cook's Notes

⏳ TIME: Preparation, including blind baking the pastry, takes about 25 minutes, cooking takes about 40 minutes.

◯ SERVING IDEAS: Serve warm or lightly chilled at buffets or picnics, as either a first or main course.

❓ VARIATION: If you cannot find saffron but like the yellow colour, you can substitute turmeric, but it will not give quite the same flavour.

AROMATIC CHICKEN CURRY

SERVES 4

This isn't quite what you'd expect from a curry, for it is not hot, yet such voluptuous flavours are more representative of Indian cooking than dishes which burn the roof of your mouth off.

8 Quality British Chicken thighs, skinned
225g/8oz onion, finely chopped
1 tbsp granulated sugar
8 whole, unpeeled garlic cloves
1 fresh lime, quartered
1 cinnamon stick
8 cardamom pods
6 whole cloves
2 sachets saffron powder, or to taste
600ml/1 pint boiling water
100g/4oz coconut cream (solid)
2-3 bananas, peeled and cut into large chunks
Salt and freshly ground black pepper

1. Cook the onion in a little oil or butter until very soft, then sprinkle over the sugar and cook over a moderate heat until it has caramelised and the onions are a good golden brown.

STEP 1

2. Add the garlic, lime, cinnamon stick, cardamom, cloves and saffron, stir well, then place the chicken pieces in the pan and pour over the water.

3. Bring to the boil, cover and simmer gently until the chicken is tender – about 30 minutes.

4. Remove the chicken and keep warm. Ideally you should take out the lime, cinnamon stick and the other whole spices.

5. Break up the coconut cream and gradually stir the pieces into the liquid, taking care not to let it boil.

STEP 5

6. Taste and adjust the seasoning – add extra coconut if you like a thicker or richer sauce, but be careful not to hide the subtle taste of the spices.

7. Return the chicken pieces to the sauce with the pieces of banana. Warm gently for a few minutes then serve.

Cook's Notes

⏱ TIME: Preparation takes about 20 minutes, cooking takes about 40 minutes.

❓ VARIATION: If you cannot find saffron but like the yellow colour, you can substitute turmeric, although it will not give quite the same flavour.

◯ SERVING IDEAS: Serve with lightly fried cashew nuts, mango chutney or natural yogurt with cucumber and mint.

ORANGE AND CARDAMOM CHICKEN WINGS

SERVES 4

The rather mysterious, perfumed flavour of cardamom is intriguing enough to use without many other ingredients, and almost everyone likes it.

8 Quality British Chicken wings
4 cloves garlic, crushed
Finely grated rind 1 large orange
6 tbsps orange juice
1 tbsp lemon juice
4 tbsps oil
Seeds from 10 cardamom pods, crushed
Salt and freshly ground black pepper

1. Wipe the chicken wings with some kitchen paper and cut off the tips. Put into a shallow ovenproof dish.

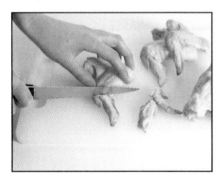

STEP 1

2. Mix the remaining ingredients together, pour over the chicken and allow to marinate for at least 4 hours, covered, at room temperature, or up to 24 hours in a refrigerator.

STEP 2

3. Cook the wings, uncovered, at 200°C/400°F/ Gas Mark 6, for about 30 minutes, basting once or twice. Serve hot or cold.

Cook's Notes

TIME: Preparation takes about 25 minutes, plus a minimum of 2 hours marinating time. Cooking takes about 45 minutes.

SERVING IDEAS: Serve on a bed of rice with stir-fried vegetables.

APRICOT CHICKEN WITH MINT

SERVES 4

This is a delicious recipe with a light, yogurt-based sauce of the most beguiling pale apricot colour and fascinating clear flavour. It can be served hot or cold.

8 Quality British Chicken thighs or drumsticks, skinned
50g/2oz onion, finely chopped
1 orange
2 tbsps lemon juice
50g/2oz dried apricots
2 tbsps chopped fresh mint or 2 tsps dried mint
150ml/¼ pint dry white wine
Salt and freshly ground black pepper

To Serve
3-4 tbsps thick natural yogurt

1. Put the chicken into a flameproof casserole and add the onion, finely grated rind of the orange with 4 tablespoons of juice, and the remaining ingredients; be generous with the mint, as much of the flavour cooks away.

STEP 1

2. Cover and marinate for 2-4 hours at room temperature, or overnight in the refrigerator.

3. Preheat the oven to 190°C/375°F/Gas Mark 5, and bake the chicken, covered, for 45 minutes.

4. Remove the chicken and keep warm.

5. Purée the rest of the casserole contents in a food processor or liquidiser and then force through a sieve (using the back of a soup ladle for efficiency and speed) into a saucepan.

STEP 5

6. Reheat but do not boil. Remove from the heat and stir in the yogurt, tasting all the time to get a pouring sauce that is rich but light in flavour – you will probably need 3-4 tablespoons of thick yogurt.

7. Adjust the seasoning with salt and pepper then pour the sauce over the chicken.

Cook's Notes

TIME: Preparation takes about 25 minutes, plus a minimum of 2 hours marinating time. Cooking takes about 45 minutes.

VARIATION: You can serve this dish cold for a buffet, in which case you should cool the chicken and the sauce separately.

SERVING IDEAS: You can serve the dish hot, with the sauce in a separate container as a dip. In both cases, it is ideal with a mixed green salad.

CURRIED CHICKEN
DRUMSTICKS

SERVES 4

This Tandoori recipe appeals to all age groups and is perfect for barbecues or for informal parties as it can be made in large quantities. Keep an eye on the chicken whilst it's cooking – it should be basted and turned frequently so that it cooks to a good, deep brown but doesn't burn.

8 Quality British Chicken drumsticks
2 lemons
4 large cloves garlic, crushed
2cm/1 inch piece of root ginger, peeled and
    finely chopped or minced
1 generous tsp ground cumin
2 tsps sweet paprika
2 tsps ground coriander
150ml/¼ pint natural yogurt
¼ tsp chilli powder or cayenne pepper

1. Wipe the drumsticks with some kitchen roll and score with a sharp knife in several places.

STEP 1

2. Sprinkle with half the lemon juice and put into a shallow dish. Mix the remaining ingredients together and spread evenly over the chicken.

STEP 2

3. Cover the dish and leave to marinate overnight in the refrigerator. Preheat the oven to 200°C/400°F/Gas Mark 6.

4. Transfer the chicken to a foil-lined baking tin and cook, uncovered, for 30 minutes, turning halfway through.

STEP 5

5. Preheat the grill to a high temperature; baste the chicken and put under the grill for 10-15 minutes, turning and basting frequently until very brown.

Cook's Notes

⏱ TIME: Preparation takes about 15 minutes, plus overnight marinating time. Cooking takes about 40-45 minutes.

❓ VARIATION: If liked, red food colouring may be added to the marinade for an authentic appearance, although this will not affect the flavour. For extra heat, add more chilli powder, or some mustard oil.

◯ SERVING IDEAS: Serve the chicken with lemon and cucumber and a dressing of natural yogurt into which you have stirred lots of chopped fresh mint.

HOT CHICKEN WITH PEACHES

SERVES 2

Tangy with fresh ginger and fruit vinegar, this combination makes a delicious summer dinner party dish.

350g/12oz boneless Quality British Chicken meat
2 tbsps fruit vinegar (or cider vinegar)
2 tbsps dry white wine
1 tbsp finely grated fresh ginger
350-450g/12-16oz fresh peaches
2 tbsps oil
1 tbsp sliced fresh mint
Salt and freshly ground black pepper

---

1. If using breast meat, cut into long, thin strips – the average breast should make 3 or 4 pieces. If using thigh or drumstick meat, keep in large pieces.

2. Put the chicken into a shallow dish with the fruit or cider vinegar and the grated ginger; cover and leave to marinate in a cool place for a few hours.

STEP 2

3. Meanwhile, drop the peaches into boiling water for two minutes, then peel and cut into segments.

STEP 3

4. Drain the marinade from the chicken and reserve.

5. Heat the oil in a pan, then add the chicken and cook over medium heat for 5-7 minutes, turning from time to time, until cooked through.

STEP 5

6. Remove the chicken to a warm dish. Pour the marinade and the wine into the pan, season and, when hot, slide in the peaches and heat through without stirring.

7. Sprinkle the mint leaves into this hot liquid and the moment they have wilted, remove the pan from the heat. Serve the chicken topped with the peaches and with the hot vinaigrette strained over the combination.

Cook's Notes

TIME: Preparation takes about 30 minutes, plus a minimum of two hours marinating time. Cooking takes about 15 minutes.

VARIATION: If you like a more savoury flavour, soften an ounce of very finely chopped onion and/or a little garlic in the oil before adding the chicken, but try not to let either burn.

SERVING IDEAS: Serve this dish on top of a mixed salad, or accompanied by a selection of plainly cooked, seasonal vegetables.

CHICKEN SALAD WITH MANGO AND SOURED CREAM DRESSING

SERVES 4

This recipe is a perfect way of turning leftover chicken into a delicious main course dish.

450g/1lb cooked Quality British Chicken
    breast, skinned and boned
4 tbsps dry white wine
2 tbsps fresh chives, chopped, or 1 tbsp dried
    chives
4 heaped tbsps good mayonnaise
4 heaped tbsps soured cream
Scant tsp powdered mustard
1-2 mangoes, depending on size (and your
    budget)
Salt and freshly ground black pepper

1. Put the chives, with 4 tablespoons of dry white wine, into a small pan and simmer, uncovered, for about 5 minutes, until reduced to only 1 or 2 tablespoons.

STEP 1

2. Pour through a fine sieve, pushing the chives to extract as much of their essence as possible.

STEP 2

3. Mix the mayonnaise with the soured cream, mustard and about 1 tablespoon of the chive essence. Don't let the dressing become too thin, particularly if the dish is being made in advance.

4. Check the seasoning, adding salt and pepper if necessary.

5. Peel and slice the mango and cut the cold chicken into slices of approximately the same size.

STEP 5

6. Arrange roughly in a shallow dish and pour the dressing over, tossing lightly so that all the pieces are covered, but not broken.

Cook's Notes

⏱ TIME: Preparation takes about 25 minutes.

○ SERVING IDEAS: This salad is delicious when served with a chilled Chardonnay wine.

CHICKEN PROVENÇAL
CASSEROLE
SERVES 6

This is a wholesome dish and very easy to prepare, since all the vegetables bake with the chicken.

1 x 1.45kg/3 ½ lb oven-ready Quality British
   Chicken
2 tbsps olive oil
300g/12oz potatoes
1 small aubergine
2 courgettes
200g/8oz large tomatoes
1 onion, peeled and sliced
2 tsps fresh thyme leaves or 1 tsp dried thyme
1 clove garlic, crushed
1 lemon
Salt and freshly ground black pepper

1. Heat the oven to 190°C/375°F/Gas Mark 5. Heat the oil in a large frying pan and fry the chicken on all sides until a golden brown.

STEP 1

2. Set aside while preparing the vegetables.

3. Peel the potatoes and slice thinly.

4. Skin the tomatoes: to do this prick the skins with a knife, plunge the tomatoes in boiling water for five seconds, then lift out and peel.

STEP 4

5. Slice the aubergine, courgettes and tomatoes across into 0.5cm/¼-inch-thick slices. In a large casserole, layer the potatoes, aubergine, courgettes, tomatoes and onions, sprinkling with thyme, crushed garlic, salt and pepper.

STEP 6

6. Push the lemon into the cavity of the chicken and lay it on top of the vegetables.

7. Pour over any oil that is left in the bottom of the frying pan and cover with a serving lid.

8. Bake for two hours, or until the vegetables are soft and the chicken is tender.

Cook's Notes

TIME: Preparation takes about 35 minutes, cooking takes about 2 hours.

VARIATION: If you prefer, you can substitute a tin of chopped tomatoes for the fresh ones.

SERVING IDEAS: Serve with a chilled dry rosé wine from Provence.

SPECIAL OCCASION CURRIED CHICKEN

SERVES 6

This recipe makes a delicious alternative to plain roasted chicken and will appeal to the whole family.

1 x 1.45kg/3½ lb oven-ready Quality British Chicken
40g/1½ oz butter
1 onion, finely chopped
2 cloves garlic, crushed
2cm/1 inch fresh root ginger, peeled and finely grated
3 level tbsps curry powder
1 small green chilli, de-seeded and finely chopped
450ml/¾ pint chicken stock
3 tbsps mango chutney
1 tbsp soft brown sugar
Juice ½ lemon
Good pinch garam masala

To Serve
Boiled rice

1. Heat the oven to 160°C/325°F/Gas Mark 3.

2. Put the chicken in a deep roasting dish or casserole which has a tight-fitting lid.

3. Heat the butter in a saucepan and sauté the onion and garlic over a gentle heat until soft.

STEP 3

4. Add the ginger, curry powder and chopped chilli and cook for two minutes.

5. Add the stock, mango chutney, sugar and lemon juice and simmer, uncovered, for 30 minutes.

STEP 5

6. Pour this sauce over the chicken, cover and cook for 2½ hours, basting the chicken occasionally with the juices in the dish. Then remove the lid and return to the oven for a further 30 minutes to allow the sauce to evaporate and thicken.

STEP 6

7. Sprinkle with garam masala and serve with boiled rice.

Cook's Notes

TIME: Preparation takes about 10 minutes, cooking takes about 3½ hours.

VARIATION: You can substitute a few drops of chilli sauce for the whole chilli.

SERVING IDEAS: As an alternative to boiled rice, serve with nan bread, with perhaps a spicy sambal, or chutney.

VENETIAN CHICKEN

SERVES 4-6

This elegant dinner party dish incorporates traditional Italian ingredients. It is a delicious recipe which can't fail to impress your guests.

400g/1lb boneless Quality British Chicken
    breasts, skinned and cut into 1cm/½ inch
    cubes
1 tbsp olive oil
25g/1oz butter
1 onion, peeled and finely sliced
2 cloves garlic, crushed
1 tsp dried oregano
200g/8oz Italian risotto rice (or long grain)
1 tbsp tomato purée
1.2 litres/2 pints good chicken stock
Splash white wine
Salt and freshly ground black pepper
6 tomatoes, skinned, de-seeded and chopped
10 pitted black olives, halved
2 tbsps chopped parsley
50g/2oz Parmesan cheese, grated

1. Heat the oil and butter in a large frying pan and fry the onion and garlic over a gentle heat until soft and lightly browned.

STEP 1

2. Add the diced chicken and cook until pale brown.

STEP 2

3. Add the oregano and rice and fry for one minute.

4. Add the tomato purée, stock and wine.

5. Season with salt and pepper and stir well. Do not be tempted to stir again during cooking, since this would make the rice sticky.

6. Cook over a very gentle heat for about 25-30 minutes, until all the stock has been absorbed but the rice still has a slight bite to it.

7. Lightly fork in the tomatoes, olives and chopped parsley, cook for two minutes and serve sprinkled with Parmesan cheese.

STEP 7

Cook's Notes

TIME: Preparation takes about 15 minutes, cooking takes about 30 minutes.

VARIATION: If you prefer, you can substitute a tin of tomatoes, drained, for the six whole tomatoes.

SERVING IDEAS: Serve with a chilled white wine – Frascati complements this dish very well.

CHICKEN IN MUSTARD AND BRANDY SAUCE

SERVES 4

This dish is a real dinner party dazzler. It tastes delicious and doesn't take long to prepare.

---

8 Quality British Chicken thighs
25g/1oz butter
5 large garlic cloves, unpeeled
5 tbsps wine vinegar
300ml/½ pint dry white wine
2 tbsps brandy
2 tsps Dijon mustard
1 heaped tsp tomato purée
300ml/½ pint double cream
2 tomatoes, skinned and de-seeded

---

1. Heat the butter in a large, heavy-based saucepan or frying pan. Fry the chicken thighs on both sides to brown them evenly. Add the unpeeled garlic cloves and reduce the heat.

STEP 1

2. Cover the pan and cook gently for 20 minutes, or until the chicken is tender.

3. Pour out all but one tablespoon of fat from the pan and add the vinegar, stirring well and scraping up any sediment from the bottom.

4. Boil rapidly until the liquid is reduced to about two tablespoons.

5. Lift out the chicken and keep warm.

6. Add the wine, brandy, mustard and tomato purée to the pan. Mix well and boil rapidly once again until reduced to a thick sauce (about 5 minutes).

STEP 7

7. In another heavy saucepan, boil the cream until reduced by half, stirring frequently to prevent it burning. Take off the heat.

8. Sieve the vinegar sauce into the cream, pressing the garlic cloves well to remove the pulp. Season with salt and black pepper.

STEP 8

9. Cut the de-seeded tomatoes into thin strips and stir into the sauce. Reheat the sauce if necessary.

10. Arrange the chicken on a hot serving dish and spoon over the sauce to serve.

Cook's Notes

⏳ TIME: Preparation takes about 25 minutes, cooking takes about 30 minutes.

❓ VARIATION: If you prefer, chicken breasts can be used rather than thighs.

🅾 SERVING IDEAS: Serve with new or sautéed potatoes and courgettes, which marry well with the flavour of Dijon mustard.

CHICKEN THIGHS IN PERNOD

SERVES 4

Your guests will feel extremely pampered when they sit down to this dish. They will think you've spent the afternoon in the kitchen, but in fact it's very easy to prepare.

8 Quality British Chicken thighs
25g/1oz butter
2 shallots, peeled and finely chopped
2 tbsps water
5 tbsps Pernod
Salt and freshly ground black pepper

1. Melt the butter in a large sauté pan or saucepan. When hot, fry the thighs for eight minutes, browning on all sides. Reduce the temperature, add the shallots and water and cover the pan.

STEP 1

2. Continue to cook slowly for another 30-35 minutes, or until the chicken portions are cooked.

3. Remove the lid, increase the temperature and pour in the Pernod.

STEP 3

4. Set alight with a match and turn off the heat. When the flames die down, scrape up any sediment from the bottom of the pan.

STEP 4

5. Remove the chicken portions to a warm serving dish. Season the remaining juices with salt and pepper and bring to the boil. Spoon over the chicken and serve.

Cook's Notes

TIME: Preparation takes about 20 minutes, cooking takes about 30-35 minutes.

SERVING IDEAS: Serve on a bed of rice with a selection of seasonal vegetables.

SPATCHCOCKED POUSSINS IN MUSTARD

SERVES 4

This is a very eye-catching dish and very simple to prepare. In fact it is one of the rare dinner party dishes that you can prepare solely under the grill.

2 double Quality British Chicken poussins
    (each about 600g/1 ½ lbs in weight)
100g/4oz butter, softened
2 tbsps wholegrain mustard
2 tsps sugar
Salt and freshly ground black pepper

To Serve
Large bunch watercress

1. Heat the grill to high.

2. To 'spatchcock' the poussins, turn each one over in turn and cut through flesh and bone from tail to neck along one side of the backbone. Then flip over so that the skin side is uppermost.

STEP 2

3. Open the bird out flat and press along the breastbone with the heel of the hand to flatten it thoroughly.

STEP 3

4. Lay the birds bony side uppermost and grill for seven to ten minutes.

STEP 5

5. Meanwhile, mix the butter with the mustard and sugar. Turn the birds over and spread with the mustard butter.

6. Season with salt and pepper and grill for another ten minutes, or until cooked through and deep brown. Serve on a large platter with watercress.

Cook's Notes

⏲ TIME: Preparation takes about 20 minutes, cooking takes about 20 minutes.

▢ SERVING IDEAS: A chilled, light white wine goes very well with this dish.

CHICKEN CALVADOS

SERVES 6

The Calvados, apples and cider used in this recipe combine to make a rich, satisfying dinner party dish which is excellent all year round.

---

6 Quality British Chicken quarters
25g/1oz butter
1 tbsp oil
1 large onion, peeled and finely sliced
1 clove garlic, crushed
1 large Bramley apple, peeled, cored and sliced
1 tsp sugar
150ml/¼ pint dry cider
1 tsp fresh thyme or ½ tsp dried thyme
Salt and freshly ground black pepper
4 tbsps Calvados
3 tbsps double cream

For the Decoration
25g/1oz butter
1 tsp sugar
2 dessert apples, peeled, cored and sliced

---

1. Melt the butter and oil in a large sauté pan and fry the chicken pieces, a few at a time, to an even, golden brown.

STEP 1

2. Remove the chicken and add the onion, garlic, Bramley apple slices and sugar to the pan.

3. Cook over a moderate heat until the apple is softened and light brown.

4. Return the chicken to the pan, pour in the cider, sprinkle in the thyme and season with salt and pepper.

5. Cover and simmer over a gentle heat for 35-40 minutes, or until the chicken is tender.

6. Remove the chicken pieces and keep warm.

7. Skim off any fat and then increase the heat and boil the sauce rapidly until thickened and reduced by half.

8. Put the Calvados into a metal soup ladle or small saucepan and warm gently.

9. Set it alight with a match. Let the flames die down and then add to the sauce.

STEP 9

10. Add the double cream to the pan and stir in.

11. Return the chicken to the pan and keep it hot over a low heat while frying the apple slices for the decoration.

12. For the decoration, heat 25g/1oz butter in a small frying pan, sprinkle in the sugar and add the apple slices in one layer. Fry until brown, turning once. Serve the chicken topped with the apple slices.

Cook's Notes

TIME: Preparation takes about 25 minutes, cooking takes about 45-50 minutes.

SERVING IDEAS: Serve with a julienne of carrots, steamed broccoli and boiled potatoes. A chilled white wine, such as Frascati, goes well with this dish.

CHICKEN WITH CORIANDER AND PILAU RICE

SERVES 4

Exotic spices used to be a frequent accompaniment to chicken dishes, and this dish combines a wide selection of spices, none of which is too way-out or fiery hot.

8 Quality British Chicken thighs
½ tbsp oil
25g/1oz butter
1 large onion, peeled and sliced
1 tsp paprika
1 tsp cumin powder
1 tsp turmeric
½ tsp dried thyme
Freshly ground black pepper
300ml/½ pint well-flavoured chicken stock
25g/1oz pitted black olives (about 10 olives)
2 tbsps finely chopped fresh coriander
Squeeze lemon juice

For the Pilau Rice
40g/1½ oz butter
50g/2oz whole blanched almonds
1 small onion, peeled and finely diced
50g/2oz sultanas or raisins
300g/12oz long grain rice
750ml/1¼ pints boiling water
½ tsp salt

1. Heat the oil and butter in a large frying pan and fry the chicken until an even golden brown colour. Transfer to a plate.

2. Add the onion to the remaining fat and fry until softened and tinged with brown.

3. Add the paprika, cumin and turmeric and fry for one minute. Add the thyme, black pepper and stock and bring to the boil.

4. Return the chicken to the pan, skin side down. Cover and simmer for 1-1¼ hours, or until the chicken is tender.

5. Remove the chicken with a slotted spoon to a warm serving dish and keep warm.

6. Reduce the sauce by boiling rapidly until it thickens. Stir in the olives, coriander and lemon juice, season to taste and spoon over the chicken.

STEP 6

7. To prepare the pilau rice, melt 15g/½ oz butter in a small pan and when hot add the almonds and fry until lightly tinged with brown.

8. Dip the base of the pan into cold water to cool it down and prevent further cooking.

9. Melt the remaining butter in a large saucepan and fry the onion over a gentle heat until softened, but not coloured.

10. Add the fried almonds, sultanas and rice and fry for one minute. Add the boiling water and salt. Bring to the boil. Cover, reduce the heat to low and simmer for 15 minutes, until all the water has been absorbed.

11. Fork the rice lightly and serve with the chicken.

Cook's Notes

TIME: Preparation takes about 20 minutes, cooking takes about 1-1¼ hours.

SERVING IDEAS: A chilled white wine from Alsace complements this dish well.

CHICKEN IN RED PEPPER SAUCE

SERVES 4

This recipe blends the exotic spices of the Far East with the delicate flavour of chicken. It's quick to prepare and is an ideal way of livening up your midweek menus.

4 large boneless Quality British Chicken
    breasts, skinned
25g/1oz butter
1 tbsp oil
1 medium onion, peeled and roughly chopped
2cm/1 inch fresh ginger, peeled
3 cloves garlic, peeled
25g/1oz blanched almonds
300g/12oz red pepper, seeded and roughly
    chopped
1 tbsp cumin powder
2 tsps coriander powder
1 tsp turmeric powder
Pinch cayenne pepper
½ tsp salt
6 tbsps vegetable oil
150ml/¼ pint water
3 star anise (a Chinese spice available in good
    supermarkets)
2 tbsps lemon juice
Freshly ground black pepper

1. Cut the chicken breasts into largish pieces about 4cm/2 inches long and 2cm/1 inch wide.

STEP 1

2. Heat the butter and oil in a frying pan, add the chicken pieces and cook for five minutes. Remove to a plate.

3. Combine the onion, ginger, garlic, almonds, red peppers, cumin, coriander, turmeric, cayenne and salt in a food processor or liquidiser.

STEP 4

4. Blend to a smooth paste. Heat the oil in a large saucepan or deep frying pan. Add the paste and fry for 10-12 minutes.

5. Add the chicken pieces, 150ml/¼ pint water, the star anise, lemon juice and black pepper. Cover, reduce the heat and simmer gently for 25 minutes, or until the chicken is tender. Stir a few times during cooking.

STEP 5

Cook's Notes

⏱ TIME: Preparation takes about 30 minutes, cooking takes about 25 minutes.

▢ SERVING IDEAS: Serve on a bed of rice.

SPICY CHICKEN

SERVES 4

This is a really aromatic dish, perfect for special midweek dinner parties.

8 Quality British Chicken thighs or drumsticks, skinned and boned
4 large dry red chillies
½ tsp cumin seed
¼ tsp fennel seed
2 tbsps coriander seed
2cm/1 inch fresh ginger, peeled and roughly chopped
1 clove garlic, roughly chopped
Juice 1 lime
Salt
2 tbsps oil

1. Soak the chillies in warm water for five minutes.

STEP 1

2. Meanwhile, put the cumin seed, fennel seed and coriander seed into a dry frying pan and fry over a high heat until the seeds become slightly coloured and give off a spicy aroma.

3. Drain the chillies and put them, with the dry roasted spices, ginger and garlic, into a food processor or pestle and mortar and grind to a paste. Then gradually add the lime juice.

STEP 3

4. Cut the chicken into 2cm/1 inch cubes, stir in the chilli paste and a pinch of salt.

5. Leave to marinate in the fridge for two hours.

6. Heat the oil in a large frying pan and fry the chicken pieces over a medium heat until firm to the touch and cooked through. Do not be tempted to overcrowd the pan – they should only be cooked in a single layer. Keep each batch warm as you do the next.

STEP 6

Cook's Notes

TIME: Preparation takes about 15 minutes, plus 2 hours chilling time. Cooking takes about 20 minutes.

SERVING IDEAS: Serve with a salad of chopped tomatoes, cucumbers and carrot on a bed of lettuce, with thick yogurt on the side.

CHICKEN WINGS WITH FRUIT GLAZE

SERVES 4

This is an ideal recipe for summer outdoor eating. Chicken wings make excellent finger food and this tangy glaze is a perfect accompaniment to the delicate chicken flavour.

12 Quality British Chicken wings

For the Glaze
2 tbsps white wine
Grated rind of 1 orange
6 tbsps orange juice
1 tbsp lemon juice
5 tbsps honey or stem ginger syrup
½ tsp ground cinnamon
1 tsp ginger powder
Salt and freshly ground pepper

1. Mix all the glaze ingredients together in a large bowl. Add the chicken wings and marinate for at least four hours, preferably overnight, in the refrigerator.

STEP 1

2. Heat the oven to 190°C/375°F/Gas Mark 5.

3. Line a large roasting tin with a double piece of foil and place in the chicken wings and glaze mixture.

STEP 3

4. Arrange the wings so that they are outer side uppermost.

5. Bake for 50 minutes to one hour, basting regularly. If the glaze is still quite liquid at the end of the cooking time pour it off into a small saucepan and boil rapidly until it thickens.

6. Spoon this back over the chicken wings. These are equally good eaten hot or cold.

STEP 6

Cook's Notes

TIME: Allow at least four hours to marinate the chicken. Preparation takes about 10 minutes, cooking takes about 1 hour.

SERVING IDEAS: For a picnic, serve with cold brown rice.

VARIATION: When in a hurry, you could substitute orange marmalade for the glaze. Simply brush the chicken wings with strained marmalade and bake as above.

HERBY LEMON CHICKEN

SERVES 4

Served either hot or cold, this refreshing recipe is perfect for picnics and light suppers.

8 Quality British Chicken drumsticks, skinned
150g/6oz fresh white breadcrumbs
2 tbsps chopped parsley
2 tbsps chopped tarragon
Zest 1 lemon
Salt and freshly ground black pepper
1 tbsp Dijon mustard
50g/2oz butter
Flour for dusting
1 egg, size 2, beaten

For the Lemon and Herb Butter
100g/4oz butter
Zest ½ lemon
Squeeze lemon juice
½ tbsp chopped parsley
½ tbsp chopped tarragon

1. Put the breadcrumbs in a large, shallow bowl and add the parsley, tarragon and lemon zest. Season with salt and pepper and mix well.

STEP 1

2. Put the mustard and butter together in a saucepan and melt. Remove from the heat and add the breadcrumb mixture, stirring well to coat all the breadcrumbs in butter. Cool.

3. Heat the oven to 200°C/400°F/Gas Mark 6.

4. Dust each drumstick with flour.

STEP 4

5. Dip into the beaten egg and then roll in the breadcrumbs, pressing the mixture on gently to give an even coating.

STEP 5

6. Lay the drumsticks on a rack over a roasting tin and bake for 30-40 minutes, or until golden and crisp. Serve with lemon and herb butter.

Cook's Notes

TIME: Preparation takes about 25 minutes, cooking takes about 30-40 minutes.

VARIATION: You could subsitute fresh brown breadcrumbs for white and experiment by using your own favourite herbs.

SERVING IDEAS: Serve hot with herb butter and a slice of lemon, or cold with a green salad.

LEFTOVER CHICKEN SALAD

SERVES 4-6

This recipe is perfect for using up leftovers of cooked chicken. It makes a delicious midweek meal but it would be equally good to serve at a cold buffet.

400g/1lb cooked Quality British Chicken meat, broken or cut into small chunks
2 ripe but firm avocados, or 1 mango
Squeeze lemon juice
4 tomatoes, skinned
2 spring onions, chopped
2 tbsps chopped parsley
50g/2oz toasted cashew nuts

For the Garlic Vinaigrette
3 tbsps groundnut oil
1 tbsp white wine vinegar
1 tsp French mustard
1 clove garlic, crushed
½ tsp caster sugar
Salt and freshly ground black pepper

---

1. Split the avocado in half, remove the stone and skin and cut the flesh into neat slices. Brush with lemon juice to prevent discolouration. If using mango instead, peel and cut the flesh into neat slices.

STEP 1

2. Slice each tomato neatly and arrange alternately with the avocado or mango around the outer edge of a flat serving dish.

3. Mix the chicken with the spring onions, parsley and nuts.

STEP 3

4. Whisk together the garlic vinaigrette ingredients and use enough to coat the chicken well. Pile the mixture in the centre of the avocado or mango and tomato.

STEP 4

5. Brush the avocado or mango and tomato with a little dressing and sprinkle everything lightly with chopped parsley.

Cook's Notes

⏰ TIME: Preparation takes about 25 minutes.

❓ VARIATION: You can always be more adventurous and use paw paws, kiwi fruit or peaches in place of the avocado.

⭕ SERVING IDEAS: Serve the salad with granary bread and butter and a chilled dry white wine.

SIMPLE CHICKEN CASSEROLE

SERVES 4

This is really a cheat's recipe – a can of soup saves a great deal of time, but the end result is delicious.

8 Quality British Chicken thighs
1 tbsp oil
25g/1oz butter
250g/10oz can condensed cream of mushroom
    soup
3 tbsps single cream
200g/8oz button mushrooms, sliced
4 tbsps dry sherry

1. Heat the oven to 190°C/375°F/Gas Mark 5.

2. Heat the oil and butter in a heavy-based frying pan and fry the chicken pieces on both sides to a golden brown.

STEP 2

3. Mix the can of soup with the sliced mushrooms, cream and sherry.

STEP 3

4. Pour over the chicken, cover and bake for 1¼-1½ hours, or until the chicken is tender.

Cook's Notes

TIME: Preparation takes about 10 minutes, cooking takes about 1¼-1½ hours.

VARIATION: You can add shallots to the sauce for more flavour.

SERVING IDEAS: Serve with sautéed potatoes and a selection of seasonal vegetables.

SPICY BARBECUE CHICKEN

SERVES 4

Whether you cook this recipe in the oven on a cold winter's evening or on the barbecue in the height of summer, it is bound to be a success.

4 Quality British Chicken portions
150ml/¼ pint maple syrup or clear honey
¼ tsp cayenne pepper
½ tsp salt
Freshly ground black pepper
2 cloves garlic, crushed
2 tbsps tomato purée
1 tbsp Dijon mustard
2 tbsps lemon juice

1. Heat the oven to 230°C/450°F/Gas Mark 8.

2. Skin the chicken joints and lay them in a roasting pan, skinned side uppermost.

STEP 2

3. Meanwhile, mix together the remaining ingredients to make the barbecue sauce.

4. Spoon enough sauce over the chicken to coat each joint well.

STEP 4

5. Bake in the oven for 30-40 minutes, basting the chicken once or twice with the sauce.

6. Serve the extra sauce separately.

Cook's Notes

TIME: Preparation takes about 10 minutes, cooking takes about 1¼-1½ hours.

VARIATION: You can use this sauce when cooking chicken portions on the barbecue. It is a good idea to marinate the chicken in the sauce for at least 4 hours before you start the barbecue, to get a really good flavour.

SERVING IDEAS: Serve with jacket potatoes and either a green salad or a selection of seasonal vegetables.

INDEX